VEGAN
DO IT!

CHARLOTTE WILLIS

WAYLAND
www.waylandbooks.co.uk

First published in Great Britain in 2020
by Wayland
Copyright © Hodder and Stoughton, 2020
All rights reserved
Editor: Julia Bird
Designer: Lisa Peacock
ISBN: 978 1 5263 1220 4
Printed in Dubai

Wayland, an imprint of Hachette Children's Group
Part of Hodder and Stoughton
Carmelite House
50 Victoria Embankment
London EC4Y 0DZ
An Hachette UK Company
www.hachette.co.uk
www.hachettechildrens.co.uk

Picture credits:
Alamy: CSU Archive/Everett Collection 6l,7tl; Oren Jack Turner/Ian Dagnellcomputing 6l.Shutterstock:A78805 11c; ArdeaStudio 7b; ArtAdi 20b; Aquamarine Painter 31t;Anatolir 37t; Annie r 45t; Dariia Baranova 47c; BeataGFX 25cla; Bestector Elements 40c;Bosotoschka 5t; BudOlga 26c; Cerama _ama 42b; Vladis Chern 15t; DaGa5 21c, 64;Dmitriylo 9b; Doremi 30t; dreamwaves 46cl; Eireann 46t; Engraving Factory 16tl;Epine 24cl; Lucia Fox 8; Foxys Graphic 14;GoodStudio 36t, 44, 61b; Happy Pictures 35t; Yuliia Husar 41t; Oleg Iatsun 20c; Indra-east 4t; Itana 47c; Iro4ka 46l; Itecheno 10c; Jemastock 38b; katieromanoff_art 28b; katrinaku 47cr;Lenjoyeverytime 25tr, 25cl; LenLis 31b, 33tr; Light_s 10b, 50t; Lineartestpilot 17tr; Lukpedclub 45b; Magic Pictures 4b; m.malinka 52; Zorana Matijasevic 16tb; Maquiladora 45c;Antonov Maxim 17br; Lorelyn Medina 13t, 19t; Melazerg 43;Messer16 20cra, 25bc; MoreVector 16-17c, 24bl, 24br, 41b; Nadia 80 53; lena_nikolaeva 11t, 18tl, 20t, 28t, 29t;Valeriya Novozhonova 27c; ONYXprj 25tl; Galyna_P 15b, 62b; Anastasia Petrova 36b, 38c; Pixsooz 39b; Garik Prost 22; Sabbracadabra 12b; Diego Schulman 12-13; Victoria Sergeeva 50b;Lilia Shlapak: 48c, 48br, 48tr, 49tl, 49cl, 49bl, 49tr, 49br, 62t; Sunnydream 25cr, 25bl;Svtdesign 39t; Mascha Tace 29c; Tartila 21b;Tutsi 40b; Arina Ulyasheva 24t, 48t; Irina Vaneeva 24cr, 25c, 25br; Svitlana Varfolomieieva 23b; Vector Dude 18cl; Vector SpMan 41c; Vectors Bang 46bl, 46br; Yury Velikanov 5b; VikiVector 21t; Andy Vinnikov 51b;Yuzach 30b. The Vegan Society 7r;

All other illustrations by Ana Seixas.

Every attempt has been made to clear copyright. Should there be any inadvertent omission please apply to the publisher for rectification.

The facts and statistics included in this book were sourced from various organisations including The Vegan Society, Veganuary, the WWF, the RSPCA, Peta and the Food and Agriculture Organization of the United Nations.

FOREWORD

WELCOME TO A NEW WAY OF LIVING! By picking up this book, you've already made an important decision – to find out more about veganism. From here, your life could transform! If you try veganism, you will come to look at plants in a completely new light, with greater insight for the health of the environment and the wellbeing of our fellow animals. All in all, being vegan is an incredibly rewarding lifestyle, and could become one of the most fantastic choices you will ever make. So, prepare to open your mind, eyes and mouth.

Let's go vegan!

CONTENTS

What is a vegan?

All vegans believe that animals are important, sentient beings who are capable of emotions and deserve to live a life free from use and exploitation. Individuals who follow a vegan lifestyle choose not to consume or use any animal products in their daily life.

> Veganism is a way of living which seeks to exclude, as far as is possible and practicable, all forms of exploitation of, and cruelty to, animals for food, clothing or any other purpose.
> – The Vegan Society

THINKING VEGAN

A vegan believes that animals do not need to suffer or die for humans to eat well, dress well and live a healthy and satisfying life. Whilst exact numbers of vegans are unknown, it is estimated that there are **MILLIONS** of vegans across the globe, with numbers growing year on year.

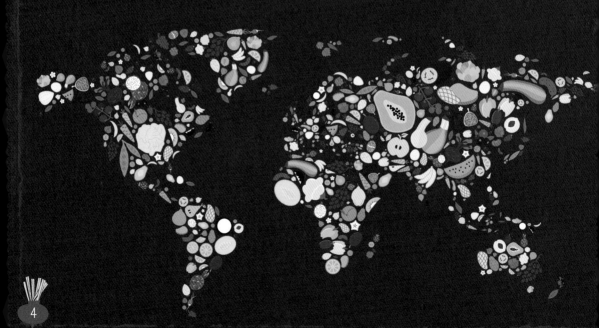

WHAT VEGANS EAT

Whilst it is necessary to know what a vegan can't eat, it is just as important to focus on the range of delicious foods that vegans **CAN** eat.

EAT UP!

Lentils, beans, pulses

Tofu, meat substitutes, faux fish products

Non-dairy milks, plant-based yogurt, dairy-free cheese

All wholegrains

All fruits

All vegetables

All nuts and seeds

Plant-based ready meals and treats

Accidentally vegan foods (such as Oreos!)

Maple syrup, agave nectar, date syrup

STEER CLEAR

Animal meat

Fish

Dairy products from animals

Eggs

Conventional cakes and ready meals

Honey

VEGANS AND VEGETARIANS: NOT THE SAME!

Vegans are different from vegetarians. Both do not eat meat or fish, but vegans omit all animal products from their diet. A vegan diet is therefore also free from dairy products, eggs and honey. Vegans also avoid eating certain food additives and ingredients (a full list can be found on page 61) and put animal welfare first when buying any products, from clothes to make-up and toiletries.

A lifestyle. Not a diet.

One of the most important things to remember if you choose to try veganism is that you are making small and meaningful changes every day towards a new lifestyle. Veganism is not, and should never be considered to be, a diet. Veganism can, in time, become an important part of your lifestyle, helping you gain a fresh perspective on your daily habits.

THE HISTORY OF VEGANISM

Despite the recent rise to fame of veganism, much thanks to social media and celebrity endorsement, a plant-based lifestyle has been a choice for some for centuries.

VEGAN HALL OF FAME

There have been many influential individuals throughout history who have spoken in favour of animal equality. Here are just some of the most noteworthy vegan or vegetarian movers, shakers and big thinkers.

ALBERT EINSTEIN (1879–1955)

'Nothing will benefit human health and increase chances for survival of life on Earth as much as the evolution to a vegetarian diet.'
Possibly the most famous scientist of all time, the brilliant Albert Einstein was an animal advocate who avoided eating meat throughout his life.

MAHATMA GANDHI (1869–1948)

Gandhi is well known for being an inspirational ethical speaker and campaigner for social justice. While choosing to be vegetarian from a young age, Ghandi became a significant figure in vegan history by avoiding consuming milk products for most of his life.

MARY SHELLEY (1797–1851)

Author of *Frankenstein*, Mary Shelley ate a meatless diet, and believed that animals should not be regarded as food for humans. In fact, if you have read *Frankenstein*, you'll know that the monster was itself vegetarian.

DONALD WATSON (1910–2005)

In 1944, Donald Watson, a keen animal rights advocate, called a meeting with five other non-dairy consuming vegetarians. These six individuals became the founders of modern veganism with the Vegan Society.

VEGANS AROUND THE WORLD

Some religions around the world unite people via the promotion of animal welfare, including Buddhism and Hinduism. Many food staples, dishes and cuisines are also already, naturally vegan. These include Asian cultures, which often favour consuming soya and pulses as a source of protein over animal products.

Modern veganism

VEGANISM IS HERE TO STAY

Anyone wanting to try veganism today will find it easier than ever before, thanks to a recent food revolution that has seen vegan products catapulted onto supermarket shelves. Veganism has come a long way in a short amount of time, making a transition to a vegan lifestyle both easier and delicious.

EVEN BEYONCÉ AND JAY-Z ARE TRYING PLANTS!

It seems like every month brings news of yet another celebrity who has decided to become vegan. Shiny new vegan ambassadors can help inspire others to discover veganism.

HERE ARE SOME CELEBRITIES WHO FOLLOW OR HAVE TRIED VEGANISM:

Billie Eilish: musician and singer
Lewis Hamilton: Formula 1 racing driver
Leonardo DiCaprio: actor, director and producer
Benedict Cumberbatch: actor
Ellie Goulding: singer and songwriter
Ariana Grande: singer, songwriter and actress
Novak Djokovic: tennis player

VEGAN OUT AND ABOUT

"I've eaten organically since I was little and always kept meat minimal but today marks my first day as a 100% Vegan!!!! Joyous day."
- Ariana Grande (@ArianaGrande)

Gone are the days when a salad or plain baked potato were your only vegan options at a restaurant or café. In almost every city, you will find vegan options at restaurants, cafés and bars. Some have their own vegan menus, with vegan-only eateries becoming popular too. Have a look online to find vegan restaurants near you.

#VEGAN

There's no doubt that social media platforms such as Facebook, Instagram and YouTube have helped people become more aware of what it means to be vegan. Just to get an idea of veganism's Insta-fame, if you perform a simple hashtag search of the term 'vegan' on Instagram, you can scroll through millions of posts!

A MODERN VEGAN LIFESTYLE

But being vegan isn't just a matter of posting about your #VeganMeal. Being a modern vegan is more about living a positive, peaceful and considered lifestyle, making conscious choices every day that make the world a better place in which to live.

VEGAN FOR HEALTH

Whilst every vegan has their own reason to change their lifestyle, there are three main reasons why individuals may find themselves drawn towards a vegan lifestyle: to enhance their health, protect the environment and help animals.

HEALTH BEGINS AT THE END OF YOUR FORK

Eating a healthy vegan diet means fuelling your body with a wholefood plant-based diet, rich in wholegrains, nuts, seeds, pulses, beans, fruits and vegetables. Processed foods (such as pre-packaged convenience and fast foods) are kept to a minimum. This approach has been scientifically proven to help promote better health, and has impressive powers when it comes to helping ward off certain diseases.

"Let thy medicine be food, and food be thy medicine."
- Hippocrates, Ancient Greek physician (c.460 BCE –375 BCE)

PLANT-BASED FIBRE

Following a wholefood plant-based diet will help you consume plenty of fibre. **SOLUBLE FIBRE** protects your heart and circulation, stabilising your blood sugar and energy levels. **INSOLUBLE FIBRE** helps the good bacteria in your gut to thrive and absorb more nutrients from your food. By eating a varied wholefood plant-based diet, you should get all the fibre you need.

An **11–16 YEAR-OLD** should eat around 25 g of fibre each day.

RICH IN ANTIOXIDANTS

Fruit and vegetables are packed full of antioxidants. These are compounds that help to protect our bodies against substances called free radicals. The presence of too many free radicals in the body is linked to illnesses such as heart disease and diabetes. The best advice? Eat a rainbow of fruit and vegetables every day.

PROTECT YOUR HEART AND BODY

Following a wholefood plant-based diet will also help to protect you from heart disease. Plant-based foods have zero cholesterol in them, while a wholefood plant-based diet has been proven to be effective at reducing bad (LDL) cholesterol in the blood, helping to stabilise blood pressure.

VEGAN FOR THE PLANET: PART ONE

Earth's precious natural resources are vanishing fast, as we cut down forests and pour pollution into the oceans and skies. The animal product industry has a big part to play in the crisis.

But there is hope. A recent United Nations report suggests that adopting a vegan diet could be one of the best ways to help preserve natural resources, prevent climate change, save water and prevent mass wildlife extinction.

THE FOREST IS BURNING

In 2019, the world looked on in horror at the huge wildfires that raged across the Amazon rainforest and Australia. It's easy to forget, however, that every single second of each day, a forest area the size of a football pitch is cleared from the rainforest to create space for animal agriculture such as beef and dairy cattle rearing, and to grow the crops to feed these animals. Whilst you've been reading this, another 1.5 to 2.5 hectares of forest has probably vanished.

BiODIVERSITY LOSS

Rainforest land reduction means the habitat loss of some of our most precious and unique wildlife. As their homes are destroyed, some species are pushed to extinction. Deforestation is to blame for the staggering daily loss of 137 rainforest species.

COMMUNITY LOSS

The displacement of indigenous people who live in the Amazon rainforest is also tragically common due to deforestation. There are over 400 indigenous groups who call the Amazon home. These groups are at serious risk, as their reservations and homes may be burned down in order to make way for animal-based land use.

AND BREATHE...

Trees and plants are like the lungs of the planet. They absorb carbon dioxide and release oxygen into the air, which we need to breathe to live. As the number of trees on Earth decreases, so too does the amount of carbon dioxide absorbed, adding to global warming (see page 14–15).

Animal agriculture is responsible for an estimated 18 per cent of total greenhouse gas emissions, the leading cause of climate change. This may not seem that huge, until you realise that all forms of travel **COMBINED** contribute just 13 per cent of greenhouse gas emissions!

VEGAN FOR THE PLANET: PART TWO

Gassy Cows

If we look at the type of greenhouse gases produced by animal agriculture, the picture gets even more concerning. Cows alone produce 150 million tonnes of methane gas every single day. Methane is even worse for the environment than carbon dioxide, as it traps heat in the atmosphere 30 times more efficiently. Methane is produced by the digestive system of cows (read: burps!) and in the fermentation of manure.

Moreover, nitrous oxide, produced by manure storage and fertilisers, has a global warming potential which is **265 TIMES** greater than carbon dioxide.

WATER, WATER, NOWHERE

Animal agriculture requires a huge amount of water to grow crops for animal feed, and for drinking water. In one day, all the humans around the world drink around 19.7 billion litres of water, while the cows involved in dairy and meat production consume around 170 billion litres of water. To put this in perspective, producing 1 kg of beef requires around 15,415 litres of water whilst 250 litres of water are needed to produce just 250 millilitres of milk.

Producing the beef for just one burger will use the equivalent of at least **20 SHOWERS'** worth of water.

OVERFISHING

If current trends in fishing and pollution continue, we could see fishless oceans become a reality by 2048. Just as we are deforesting the Amazon rainforest, we are actively destroying and overfishing our waters. Each year, as many as 100 million fish are pulled from the oceans of the world. This is an alarmingly high rate which the oceans simply can't sustain.

MODERN FISHING METHODS MEANS SHARKS, DOLPHINS AND TURTLES ARE OFTEN ACCIDENTALLY CAUGHT AND DUMPED BACK INTO THE SEAS, SOME ALREADY DEAD.

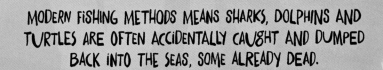

AGRICULTURE'S DEEP IMPACT

{ **W**ant to know more about farming and fishing's impact on the natural world? Here are some fast facts to chew over. }

Meat consumption is one of the leading causes of species extinction around the world.

Emissions produced from agriculture are projected to increase by 80% before the year 2050.

The average dairy farm, with 2,500 cows, produces the same amount of waste as a city with over 400,000 people living in it.

For every 1 kg of fish caught, there are up to 5 kg of marine animals caught and discarded as by-catch. This includes sharks, dolphins and turtles.

The world's meat and dairy cattle consume a quantity of food which is equal to the calorific needs of 8.7 billion people - more than the entire human population at present. Yet at any time there are millions of people facing starvation.

Producing protein from chickens requires three times as much land as producing protein from soya beans. Beef requires up to 32 times more land.

Roughly 1/3 of the planet is either desertified or severely at risk of becoming dehydrated due to water demands and climate change. Animal agriculture and livestock production is the largest driver of our global water issue.

An estimated 1/3 of the world's ice-free land is given over to animal agriculture.

Vegan for the animals: part one

FOOD ANIMAL LIFE SPAN VS NORMAL LIFE SPAN

Chickens used for meat
6 weeks vs **8** years

Lambs
6-8 months vs **12** years

Pigs
6 months vs **12** years

Cows used for milk
6 years vs **20** years

Cows used for meat
18 months vs **20** years

For the majority of us growing up, eating meat was normal. When you begin to think like a vegan, following the advice of your heart and head over your stomach and taste buds, you begin to realise that all animals are deserving of our protection and care.

ANIMALS SUFFER AND FEEL PAIN

Mammals including pigs, sheep and cows all have the same nervous system and pain receptors as we do. These animals are likely to experience pain in a similar way to humans. During their lives as a part of the animal-product industry, many animals are frequently subjected to cruel treatment. All animals involved in the food production line will also have their lives cut prematurely short (see left).

KEEPING ANIMALS CONFINED

Animals destined for our plates are, more often than not, held in cramped and confined artificial environments. For example, pigs are often held inside small pens with concrete flooring, whilst chickens are kept in sheds where thousands of birds are found under one roof. These crowded living conditions can cause anxiety and stress. What's more, in order to prevent animals from hurting one another out of sheer desperation, they are often subjected to teeth and beak clipping, a procedure carried out without painkilling medicine.

FISH HAVE FEELINGS TOO!

You might be surprised to learn that fish feel pain. Eating fish is not considered to be vegan, as fish are animals in their own right that live sentient lives and form part of a precious and vulnerable underwater ecosystem. Fish are also often caught and brought onto land whilst they are still alive, meaning that they practically suffocate before being processed and sold.

Vegan for the animals: part two

Many vegetarians would agree that the meat and fish industries are cruel. However, vegetarians may not find fault with the dairy and egg industries. There is a common misconception that no animals are killed or harmed during egg and milk production.

DAIRY IS PRETTY SCARY

Just as human mothers produce milk for their infants, mother cows have to be pregnant and give birth to a calf to produce milk. The dairy industry artificially impregnates millions of cows every year to harvest their milk. Dairy cows also have a shorter lifespan than normal, due to sheer exhaustion from continuous cycles of being pregnant and giving birth.

REARED FOR MILK AND MEAT

A mother cow and her baby are separated **WITHIN 24 HOURS** to prevent the calf from drinking the mother's milk. Female calves will usually be brought up to become dairy cattle, with male calves are slaughtered, and their meat made into pet food or other cheap animal products. Some calves are reared for veal meat and slaughtered within **18 WEEKS** of being born.

EGG INDUSTRY SECRETS

Modern supermarkets stock a range of eggs. But when we look past the marketing and focus on the life of these chickens, regardless of the eggs' classification and cost, they all face the same fate.

The vast majority of chickens will rarely see daylight, and are confined in crowded houses and sheds. Many hens' beaks are cut off in order to prevent aggressive behaviour. Commercial hens are slaughtered after only one year of life. Male chicks face a rather bleak fate. They are no use to the egg or meat industries, and are slaughtered within a few hours of hatching, using inhumane methods.

FARMERS WHO CHOOSE COMPASSION

Times are changing, and farmers are beginning to realise that sending animals to slaughter is not the only way to have a successful farming business. A former beef and dairy farmer, Jay Wilde, decided to donate his cattle to a local animal sanctuary before beginning life again as an organic vegan farmer.

Prepare

Now you've explored some of the motivating factors, you may have decided to give veganism a try. Whilst some people find success in going vegan overnight, it's often those who plan and research a vegan diet properly who make the heathiest and most sustained lifestyle changes. These four simple steps might help to guide you.

STEP 1: TELL SOMEONE!

This sounds silly, but making your decision public actually makes you more likely to stick to it. By talking with your friend or family about your lifestyle transformation, you'll re-affirm your reasons for becoming vegan, and help earn their support. They may even be tempted to give veganism a try with you.

STEP 2: KNOW YOUR 'WHY' REASONING

It is important that you know your motivation behind your decision to become a vegan. If it helps you, you can write it down in a journal, diary or on your phone to remind you of why you decided to become a vegan. This will be useful to have on hand if anyone starts offering you non-vegan food items, or you find yourself craving something non-vegan.

STEP 3: GET SAVVY ON VITAMINS AND SUPPLEMENTS

A detailed overview of the supplements you may want to consider taking can be found in Chapter 4 of this book. Very briefly, you'll want to supplement with a daily source of Vitamin D and a weekly (or daily) vitamin B12 supplement. Advice on dosage is given in Chapter 4, and will also be available from your local pharmacist or health adviser.

Step 4: Do a food shop!

Before you go vegan, you'll want to grab yourself some essential vegan ingredients and substitutions to ensure that your transition is as smooth as possible. See the next page for some of the basics you'll want to have in stock, as well as some recommendations for your first vegan shop.

WHAT TO BUY

Your first visit to the local shop or supermarket as a vegan might feel a bit strange, especially if you are used to buying meat and dairy products! Here are some handy tips on what to put into your basket or trolley.

FRESH FRUIT AND VEG

Fill up with as much fresh produce as you can. The greater the variety of colour you can squeeze into your shop, the better for your health. Choose a mixture of fruit and vegetables, ensuring you get your hands on:

Avocados
Potatoes (sweet or regular, whichever you prefer)
Berries (either blueberries, strawberries, blackberries or raspberries -
you can also get these frozen)
Bananas
Fresh garlic and herbs
Onions · Broccoli
Leafy greens such as kale, spinach and cabbage

MEAT, FISH AND DAIRY ALTERNATIVES

Replacing milk, fish and meat can be as simple as buying like-for-like alternatives. These animal-free swaps will help ease you into your vegan lifestyle. Those marked with an * should be consumed in smaller quantities:

Tofu · Tempeh
Meat-free sausages, burgers, mock-meats such as 'chick'n' and mince*
Fish-less fingers* · Dairy-free cheese*
Dairy-free milk alternatives (such as soya, oat, coconut and rice)
Dairy-free butters and spreads*
Dairy-free yogurts made using nuts, oats or soya
Vegan dips such as hummus, salsa and guacamole

FOR THE CUPBOARD

Stock up on canned beans, pulses and legumes, as well as
wholegrains such as rice, pasta and quinoa:

Canned chickpeas, black beans, kidney beans and lentils
Dried beans and pulses
Wholegrain pasta
Grains such as rice, quinoa and bulgar wheat
Oats
Cans of chopped tomatoes
Tomato puree
Cans of baked beans

BAKERY AND MISCELLANEOUS

Wholegrain bread (make sure it is labelled as vegan)
Peanut butter or a nut-butter
Marmite or similar yeast extract spread
Vegan snack bars
Nuts and seeds (at least two types)
Nutritional yeast flakes
Soya sauce
Dried fruits such as figs, apricots
and cranberries

You'll also want to check out free-from aisles in
your local supermarket, as you'll find a host of vegan
goodies hiding here! Don't forget to look in the
vegetarian frozen aisles too, there will be plenty of
vegan substitutes and staples to uncover.

DAY BY DAY

With so much to do, so much to eat, and big changes to make, you may wonder where your vegan journey should begin. In order to help you structure it, breaking your tasks and choices down into small, personal goals will help you to stay focused.

START SMALL...
AIM BIG!

The smallest changes can make the biggest and most important impact. For example, swapping your daily cereal milk (approximately 200 ml per day) from cow's milk to a plant-based alternative such as oat milk, can save almost two tennis courts' worth of grazing land every year. Choosing to eat beans and legumes, as opposed to meat and fish, can save the lives of up to 100 animals every year. If launching into a vegan diet seems overwhelming, aim to swap one animal foodstuff for a plant-based alternative each week.

DO YOUR RESEARCH

There are plenty of great resources to help support and guide you on your vegan journey. Check out some of the vegan charity websites such as Viva!, Veganuary and The Vegan Society for expert advice and use online blogs to source advice from veteran vegans. Get some recipe inspiration by searching through vegan cookery books, recipe blogs and vegan influencer pages on social media. Then try out some new recipes for yourself!

STRAWBERRY SMOOTHIE

Cook some tasty foods

The easiest way to ensure that you stay vegan is to follow your stomach! Eating a variety of delicious, plant-based meals every day will satisfy your hunger and maintain your interest in discovering this new way of living. Be as creative and inventive in the kitchen as you like, and don't be put off when things don't go exactly to plan. Turn to pages 54–59 to delve straight into some vegan eats you can create in your very own kitchen.

100% plant-based

Staying Vegan

STAY ON TRACK

It can be difficult to maintain your plant-based commitment when you are faced with meat and dairy products you used to love. Here's where your 'why' reasoning from p.23 comes into play. During moments of temptation, it is important to remember the reasons behind your switch to veganism.

WHAT IF I MAKE A MISTAKE?

Imagine you've been queuing for a hot drink for what feels like ages. You finally take a sip – and realise you forgot to order a plant-based milk alternative. You've made a mistake, now what? First of all, don't panic. Little slip-ups are natural and are part of forming successful new habits. Some mistakes can be difficult to swallow (literally!) but they do not define you. Instead, it is important to make a mental effort to avoid making the same mistake again.

WHAT ABOUT MY NON-VEGAN FOODS?

You're almost guaranteed to have some non-vegan foods lurking in your fridge or cupboards after making the decision to go vegan. Here are some of your options when it comes to non-vegan foods:

- **DONATE:** Give your unopened packets, tins and boxes of longer-life foods (such as cereals or tins of tuna) to a foodbank.

- **GIFT:** Give the unwanted foods to your friends, neighbours or flatmates.

- **GET ONLINE:** Apps such as OLIO can help local people in your area find your unwanted foods. It's like Gumtree or Craigslist, but for food.

ALTERNATIVES ARE EVERYWHERE!

You should be able to find an abundant supply of delicious vegan substitutions for favourite dishes at your supermarket, online and at health-food shops. Here are some brilliant swaps:

SWAP OUT	SWAP INSTEAD
Bacon	Aubergine Bac'n, Coconut Bac'n or pre-made Bac'n alternatives
Traditional cheeses	Pre-made coconut oil/soya-based cheezes
Meats	Vegan meat-replacements, tofu and seitan
Traditional cakes	'Free-from' and vegan cakes
Traditional ice cream	Vegan ice creams using soy, nut or oat milk

LIVING IN A NON-VEGAN HOUSE

Most vegans have non-vegan families. It can be difficult when your closest ones aren't involved in your vegan lifestyle, but don't let this deter you. Your family could even be potential vegans, ready to learn from you! Until then, here are some tips on living together.

TELL YOUR FAMILY

If you're unsure as to how your family will respond to the idea of you going vegan, here are some suggestions:
- Arm yourself with the facts. Download some key facts about veganism using leaflets from Veganuary and The Vegan Society.
- Cook them a delicious, nutritious vegan meal.
- Go out to a vegan restaurant to showcase how delicious and diverse vegan food can be.
- Show them a vegan film – documentaries such as *Cowspiracy*, *The Game Changers* and *Vegucated* can help clarify your decision to try veganism.

Later, you can perhaps ask your family to sample veganism with you – challenge them to try going plant-based for a month and share the journey together.

Veganise non-vegan dishes

Non-vegan family members, especially those who love cooking, can be concerned about cooking vegan meals. Make the process as simple as possible by 'veganising' dishes. Use vegan cheese and a plant-based milk to veganise a 'mac and cheese', use plant-based burgers and sausages at barbecues, switch meat for substitutes such as legumes when making curries, casseroles and hot-pots. Simple swaps will make your transition as effortless as possible, and help to encourage family members to try vegan versions of their classic recipes.

THE SCEPTICS

There may sometimes be the odd comment thrown around by your family members about your decision to try veganism, some of whom may be doing so out of concern for you or may be doubtful of your choice. Don't be put off by these comments. Instead, educate yourself around the topic. Arm yourself with some key facts about veganism's environmental and nutritional advantages, as well as how it benefits animal welfare.

EAT VEGAN

{ **M**aking sure you eat a balanced vegan diet is pretty straightforward, once you get some practice. Just follow some simple rules as to what you need to eat every day to help you enjoy a healthy and nourishing vegan diet. }

Mix it up

- The base of your meals should be a variety of carbohydrates, such as brown rice, pasta and wholemeal bread, as these are a healthy source of energy.

- On top of your grains, be sure to eat at least two portions (that's about a handful) of beans, pulses, lentils or legumes every day.

- You should aim to eat as many portions of vegetables as you can (especially the green, leafy ones), along with three or four portions of fruit.

- A handful of nuts and seeds. This can be peanut butter, pumpkin seeds, brazil nuts, cashews or any type of nut and seed you like!

- Getting your protein at every meal is as simple as peas (literally). Some fantastic vegan protein sources include beans, peas, lentils, tofu, tempeh and seitan.

VEGETABLES

FRUIT

☆ BE THE HEALTHIEST YOU ☆

By following a vegan diet, you're already helping to transform your body into the healthiest version it can be, so great job! To make sure you support your body, you need to eat enough plant-based sources of the essential nutrients such as calcium, iron, zinc, vitamin B12 and omegas 3 and 6. We'll show you how in this chapter.

BREAD, RICE AND PASTA

NUTS, SEEDS AND TOFU

MAKE MEALS EXCITING!

Falling in love with vegan food is easy. Making your food as tasty as possible begins with following some simple recipes, such as the ones featured on pages 54–59, and taste-testing your way through some new foods, before finding your favourite new flavours. If every mealtime is an experiment, you'll never get bored of eating delicious vegan foods!

Nutrition 101

Nutrition, or eating healthily, is an important part of being a vegan. Your body requires a certain amount of vitamins and minerals in order to work correctly. But remember, any supplementation needs to be considered alongside the advice of a healthcare professional or pharmacist to ensure the correct dosage for you.

Here's the low down of what you need to know, and where you can get each of the essential vitamins and minerals from:

VITAMIN D

Why do I need it? Vitamin D is essential for maintaining the health of the skin, the immune system and, most importantly, the bones. Vitamin D is produced by your skin in reaction to sunlight, which means that everyone in the UK needs to supplement with Vitamin D, especially in the dark months of autumn and winter.
How do I get it? Vitamin D can be sourced from mushrooms, and some fortified foods such as vegan spread and some plant-based milks. However, the most reliable source of vitamin D is in the form of a tablet or a vitamin spray, which can be bought from your local chemist or health shop.
How much? Aim for 10 mcg per day.

TAKE NOTE: Not all vitamin D supplements are vegan, as some are derived from lamb's wool. Check the vegan certification of the supplement before you buy.

VITAMIN B12

Why do I need it? Your body needs vitamin B12 for your nervous system and brain to communicate effectively, as well as allowing oxygen to travel around your body.

How do I get it? Vitamin B12 can be found in certain fortified vegan foods, such as nutritional yeast, certain plant-based milks, fortified breakfast cereals and yeast spreads. You can also supplement this with a daily or weekly B12 tablet or vitamin mouth spray.

How much? You should aim to eat fortified foods, like the ones listed above, at least twice a day. If supplementing, aim for 10 mcg per day in a tablet or spray form.

CALCIUM

Why do I need it? For strong bones, healthy teeth and proper functioning of your heart and muscles. Calcium is used all over the body, making it one of the most essential minerals to eat.

How do I get it? Eating enough calcium on a vegan diet is really easy! Certain tofu products are set, or hardened, with calcium, whilst plant-based milks, yogurts and breads are often fortified with calcium. Natural sources include kale, broccoli, Brussels sprouts, dried figs, chia seeds and almonds.

How much? Try to eat a calcium-rich food at every meal. For example, have fortified plant milk with your breakfast cereal, two slices of fortified bread for your lunchtime sandwich, snack on almond butter and fresh fruit and try steamed kale with your dinner.

OMEGA 3 AND 6

Why do I need them?

These are essential fatty acids which are used for a variety of tasks and functions in your body, from transporting hormones to maintaining healthy eyes.

How do I get them?

By eating a varied plant-based diet, rich in a variety of foods. Great sources include ground chia, flax and hemp seeds, walnuts and rapeseed oil.

How much?

Eating 1 tablespoon of ground chia seeds or linseeds and cooking with rapeseed oil should guarantee that you get enough omega 3 and 6. Try sprinkling your ground seeds onto soya yogurt or a kale salad, or use them in a smoothie, porridge or flapjack recipe.

IRON

Why do I need it?

Iron works alongside vitamin B12 in a tag team to help oxygen travel around your body, and deliver oxygen to your muscles and cells.

How do I get it?

There are plenty of plant-based sources of iron! Lentils, chickpeas, beans, cashew nuts, raisins, dried figs, tofu, quinoa, kale and pumpkin seeds all contain iron. It is important to eat a source of vitamin C, such as broccoli, oranges, tomatoes and peppers, alongside your iron-rich foods to help the iron get absorbed into your body.

How much?

Try to eat at least three to four iron-rich foods every day. Aim for one or two iron-dense portions at each main meal where possible.

IODINE

Why do I need it?
Iodine is a mineral which is essential for hormone transport and production.

How do I get it?
Iodine is passed from the soil into the vegetables and fruits we eat. However, there's no way of telling how much iodine is in each food, which presents us with a problem! The best solution is to take a regular supplement.

How much?
People over the age of 16 should get around 140 mcg of iodine per day. It is advised that you consult with a doctor, pharmacist or healthcare provider before supplementing with iodine to ensure that the dose is healthy and appropriate for you.

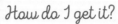

ZINC

Why do I need it?
Zinc is used for a variety of reasons within our bodies. We use zinc to fight infections, maintain healthy nails and skin, and grow.

How do I get it?
Zinc is quite easy to find in vegan foods. Chickpeas, beans, tofu, walnuts, pumpkin seeds, hemp seeds, wholewheat bread and quinoa are all brilliant sources.

How much?
Aim to eat at least two sources of zinc-rich foods every day where possible. This can be as simple as buying a seeded bread, throwing hemp seeds into your smoothies and using quinoa instead of rice.

Healthy Eating

So, now we know exactly where to get our essential vitamins, minerals and healthy fats from, let's look at an average day of eating as a vegan.

Breakfast: Porridge made with fortified plant milk (such as soya or oat), with a variety of toppings such as walnuts, ground chia seeds, dried figs and banana

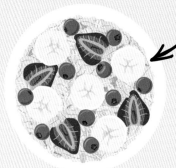

Lunch: Chickpea and tofu-mayonnaise sandwich on fortified wholemeal bread, served with a side of kale coleslaw or watercress and mixed leaf salad sprinkled with nutritional yeast and rapeseed oil dressing. One or two servings of fruit

Snacks: Peanut or almond butter on oatcakes, a handful of almonds, vegan-fortified yogurt-alternative with raisins and cashews

Dinner: Mixed bean and vegetable chilli served with lemony quinoa, avocado and fresh coriander. Side of steamed or pan-fried leafy green vegetables

YOU CAN USE THIS MEAL PLAN AS A BASIC GUIDE TO HELP YOU ON YOUR WAY TO EATING A HEALTHY VEGAN DIET AND ADAPT IT ACCORDING TO YOUR TASTES.

Every Day

PLANTS HAVE PROTEIN!

You'll soon find out that no one has ever been more interested in your protein intake than when you tell them you are vegan! People sometimes forget that plants have protein, and some of the strongest animals on Earth are plant-eaters. You'll never have to worry about getting enough protein as long as you eat a varied plant-based diet, rich in beans, tofu, green vegetables, nuts and seeds. It's that simple. Besides, cows, sheep, pigs and chickens all get their protein from plants in the first place!

MEAT REPLACEMENTS

As you have seen, there are lots of imitation meat products. These have a similar flavour and texture to traditional meat products such as bacon and burgers, but involve no animal suffering and are kinder to the environment. You can now buy meat-free mince, animal-free chicken and fish-less fingers in almost every major supermarket. While these replacements are fantastic to enjoy every now and again, try limiting your intake to two or three portions per week, as these products are sometimes high in saturated (unhealthy) fats.

SUPER SWAPS

When you first go vegan, it can be useful to make simple, like-for-like swaps of staple ingredients. These foods can make the process of becoming vegan easier for you, and will help you feel like you're not missing out on any of your favourite foods (so no FOMO!).

EGG ALTERNATIVES ☆ (BAKING) ☆

* Chia seeds - 1 tbsp chia seeds + 1 tbsp water to make a chia 'egg'
* Flax seeds - 1 tbsp flax seeds + 1 tbsp water to make a flax 'egg'
* Apple sauce
* Mashed banana
* Raising agents e.g. bicarbonate of soda
* Aquafaba (chickpea water)
* Chickpea flour (for omelettes, quiches, savoury pancakes, flans)

MILK & DAIRY ALTERNATIVES

* Soya (all-rounder)
* Hemp (nutty taste, quite distinctive)
* Rice (sweet, brilliant for coffee and tea)
* Coconut (best for baking or smoothies)
* Almond (all-rounder)
* Cashew (creamy and indulgent)
* Oat (best for hot drinks)
* Hazelnut (nutty flavour)

Cheeses

Store-bought alternatives made using coconut oil and soya come in a range of flavours. Nutritional yeast flakes (sometimes called nooch) are dried, cheesy-flavoured flakes which can be stirred into a sauce or sprinkled on top of dishes.

DITCH THE MEAT

The following are all fantastic plant-based alternatives to meat:

* Legumes (such as chickpeas, lentils, black beans, butter beans, kidney beans and edamame)
* Tofu (best for oriental cooking, stir-fry, grilling, BBQ-ing and in salads)
* Tempeh (best for oriental cooking, stir-fry, grilling, marinating and in burgers, 'meatballs' and burritos)
* Quorn/Mycoprotein (can be used in a range of dishes. Make sure it does not contain egg.)
* Soya-based meat alternatives (these include chicken-style pieces, beef-less mince and pork-free slices)
* Seitan (made using gluten - can be used in burgers, burritos, 'roast' alternatives and curries)
* Jackfruit (works best as an imitation fish, chicken or pork substitute)

KEEP THE FISH IN THE OCEAN

Fish is also easily replaced with the help of some clever substitutions and some handy seasoning. Try:

* Smoked carrot 'salmon'
* Chickpea 'tuna' (use edible seaweed such as nori to flavour the mixture)
* Tof-ish (tofu made into fish alternatives)
* Fish-free products (such as fish-less fillets, fish-free fingers and fish-less tuna cans)

HOW ABOUT HONEY?

Honey is not considered to be a part of a vegan diet as, honey is made by hardworking bees, and is often the only food source for a bee hive during the winter months. Vegan alternatives include date syrup, maple syrup and agave nectar.

Ethical beauty and clean cosmetics

Being vegan is a way of life, not just a way of eating. From washing your face with cruelty-free soaps, to putting on your vintage jacket and using a reusable straw for your smoothie, small, everyday decisions will help you to become a more successful and confident vegan.

KIND SKINCARE

Did you know that there are hidden animal-based ingredients in many skincare products? What's more, certain brands continue to use animals when testing and trialling the safety of their products. Skincare which contains animal ingredients, or has been tested on animals, is not considered vegan. Where possible, look for the Vegan Society's official certification logo (right) to ensure that the product you are purchasing is free of animals and free from cruelty. If in doubt, do a quick search online.

UGLY MAKE-UP

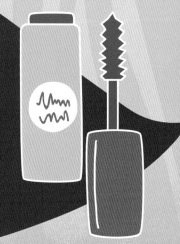

The lipstick people smear on their lips and the powders they brush and contour with every day may well contain animal ingredients. Some of the most bizarre ingredients that have been discovered in make-up include fish scales in shimmering eye shadows and crushed beetle colouring in lip tints! Buying vegan make-up is now easier than ever. Brands such as KVD, E.L.F, Inika and Lime Crime are all brilliantly vegan and are also free from animal testing.

Perfumes

Certain perfumes are also not suitable for vegans. Honey and other non-vegan ingredients can be found lurking in certain bottles, with manufacturers rarely listing their ingredients on packaging. Luckily, there are some wonderful vegan perfume companies online, and a range of resources such as vegan beauty and skincare vlogs and blogs. These will help you decide which brands to invest in.

★ CHOOSE PLASTIC-FREE ★

Many make-up brushes, cosmetics, shampoos and conditioners are packaged within plastic containers. Great for the store shelf, but less so for the environment. Try, where you can, to use plastic-free or waste-free alternatives such as soap bars, shampoo and conditioning bars, and ecologically-friendly brushes and make-up tools. Lush and The Body Shop also now offer a container recycling or refill service for certain products.

STILL CONFUSED ABOUT WHAT TO BUY?

Try finding vegan cosmetic, skincare and lifestyle bloggers and vloggers online or via social media to help you decide which brands to purchase.

SUSTAINABLE FASHION

Helping to secure the future of the environment has never been more important. The fashion industry is one of the most polluting in the world, but one which is almost entirely driven by us, the buyers. We can all help to reduce the harmful impact of the fashion industry.

WHAT IS FAST FASHION?

'Fast fashion' is a term used to describe the quickly changing trends in the fashion industry, which lead retailers to produce cheap, on-trend clothes. Fast fashion can result in a throw-away attitude towards cheaper clothing items, and all this continuous producing, buying and throwing away is very harmful to the environment.

In the last 15 years, the amount of clothes produced has doubled. In the UK alone £140 million of clothing is sent to landfill sites every year! Not only is this wasteful, but around 1.2 billion tonnes of carbon dioxide is also produced by the textile industry per year, adding to global warming. As a result, fast fashion is not considered part of a conscious and ethical lifestyle.

BUY SUSTAINABLY

To reduce the impact of your clothes upon the planet, consider how much you will use something before you buy it. Choose your clothes carefully, and try to buy from sustainable retailers where possible. Buying from vintage stores, online second-hand clothing sites such as Depop and Ebay, as well as re-inventing old clothes, are all great ways to prevent waste.

WHY NOT LEATHER AND FUR?

Leather, feathers, sheep's wool, angora wool (from angora rabbits) and fur are not vegan. This is because these materials are taken from animals, using inhumane methods. These materials should all be avoided when shopping.

You may not believe it, but there are some fantastic alternatives to leather! Here are some of the best substitutes around:

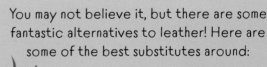

Pineapple skins - Mushroom skins
Cork - Recycled tyres
Coconut fibres - Apple fibres
Recycled bottles - Tree bark

Being social

{ Eating out and about can be more challenging when you're a vegan, but with the right preparation, there's no need to feel like you're missing out. }

☆ PARTY TIME ☆

So, you're having a few friends around! Whatever your level of cookery skill, there's an option to suit you.

Can't cook, won't cook

Source some ready-made vegan goodies. A mix of vegan dips with veggie crisps and pittas, pre-made vegan pizzas and plant-based burgers and sausages are all perfect for a simple get-together.

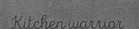

Kitchen warrior

Up for a challenge? Showcase vegan food by cooking up a show-stopping meal, such as coconut curry with rice, sautéed vegetables and sweetcorn patties, or vegan burgers piled high with melting vegan cheeze, vegan bac'n slices and grilled mushrooms.

Keen amateur

Try some simple recipes. Think stir-fry, giant salads with tempeh and tofu, homemade guacamole bruschetta and easy desserts such as a baked chocolate brownie.

Sweet treats

For dessert, whip up an apple pie using vegan pastry or get creative with home-made chocolates.

BE THE PERFECT GUEST

If you're invited to a get-together, be sure to let your host know of your dietary requirements in advance. You could suggest a simple recipe or a meat-free substitute meal for them to create. Alternatively, why not bring along your own dish? Big pots of pasta, a vegan pie or some spiced lentil cakes will all be welcomed.

SPECIAL OCCASIONS

When it comes to special meals such as at Christmas or Thanksgiving, swaps such as Tofurkey (a tofu-based turkey substitute) are perfect. Side dishes can also be easily veganised using dairy-free alternatives. Ensure your gravy is vegan by using veggie stock and use plant-based recipes to make mince pies, Christmas pudding, pumpkin pies and other seasonal treats.

HOLIDAYS

Wherever you are going on your holidays, research the available vegan options in the local area before you go. If you're staying in a hotel or BNB, make sure you inform your host of your veganism before you go. To prevent anything being lost in translation, download the Vegan Society's Vegan Passport app, which allows common vegan phrases such as "I am a vegan" and "No milk please" to be translated into 79 different languages.

FREQUENTLY ASKED QUESTIONS

If you decide to go vegan, be prepared to be asked lots of questions! Here are just a few of the most common ones.

ARE VEGANS HEALTHY?

Vegans are as healthy as they want to be! As with any diet, a vegan can choose to live off convenience or fast foods such as vegan pizza and chips, or pre-made vegan ready-meals, but these foods are often high in fats and salt and are not the best for your health. The healthiest vegan diets are those which balance eating plenty of wholefoods, such as beans, legumes and grains, with plenty of fruit and vegetables.

DO VEGANS EAT ENOUGH PROTEIN?

Yes indeed! Vegans who eat at least two portions of beans, legumes and minimally-processed soya products such as tofu and tempeh every day will be sure to get enough protein. There is also protein in vegetables, wholegrains, nuts and seeds.

HOW DO I COOK TOFU?

Tofu comes in many shapes and sizes, so how you'll want to cook your tofu depends on the type you buy. Harder tofu should be drained and pressed between tea towels and heavy books (or using a tofu press) for 20–40 mins to remove excess moisture, before being marinated for at least 30 mins with seasoning. When cooking with softer tofu, you won't need to drain as much water or marinade for as long. Follow your recipe instructions.

HOW DO I TELL MY FAMILY I'VE GONE VEGAN?

Telling your family about your transition towards a vegan diet can seem a little intimidating at first. The best way to ease any tension or difficulty is to be as honest and open about your reasoning as you can. Have a calm conversation with your family about your decision, and allow them to ask as many or as few questions as they like. It's also perfectly okay to not have all of the answers right away!

CAN I EAT VEGAN AT SCHOOL OR COLLEGE?

Yes, absolutely. If your school or college doesn't offer a vegan option, talk to your teacher about bringing in your own meals to eat at lunchtimes.

The best of the vegan myths!

VEGANS ONLY EAT SALAD

This is just not true! As you will be able to see from the incredible recipes in this book, and from your research online, vegan food knows no bounds.

ANIMALS AREN'T THE SAME AS US

While it is true that animals are not the same as humans in their biological make-up, many animals have the ability to perceive emotions, recognise faces and experience fear and grief, as well as joy and happiness. Vegans make the active decision to treat all animals, regardless of species, with the same level of respect as we would treat fellow humans – this is why vegans choose to protect animals.

FISH DON'T FEEL PAIN

Fish have been scientifically proven to have a very similar pain detection system to humans. Whilst we can't say for sure that fish experience pain in the exact same way we do, scientists are confident that they are able to detect pain, and do their best to avoid experiencing it. Fish also suffocate due to lack of water upon being caught, an experience which many believe to be painful for them.

IF WE DON'T MILK COWS, THEY'LL EXPLODE!

This is very false! Cows do not spontaneously produce milk, rather, they produce milk in response to being pregnant and giving birth to a calf. If humans did not milk the mother cow, the calf would be able to drink their mother's milk (which they are naturally meant to do – humans are not baby cows, after all), and no mother cows would be separated from their young.

IF WE ALL WENT VEGAN OVERNIGHT, WE'D BE OVERRUN WITH ANIMALS

If the world went vegan tomorrow, we would not be overrun. The animals that are caught up in the food production system would live out the rest of their lives, some of them in animal sanctuaries, without the fear of death or harm. The rate of animal births would decrease due to the lack of demand from the meat, dairy and egg industries, and the animal population would eventually reach a harmonious balance.

ISN'T IT REALLY EXPENSIVE TO BE VEGAN?

Whilst swapping like-for-like meat substitutes may be the simplest way to be vegan, it definitely won't be the most cost-effective. Meat replacements are often expensive to buy, compared to other sources of plant-based nutrition and protein, such as beans and legumes. A vegan diet that focuses on eating wholefoods is cheaper than an omnivorous diet, providing processed vegan products are kept to a minimum.

DON'T PLANTS HAVE FEELINGS TOO?

Plants, unlike animals, do not possess a nervous system which is capable of detecting pain. Nor do plants have brains, blood vessels or any consciousness, level of thought or ability to feel emotions. So, nope. Plants don't have feelings.

BUT AREN'T WE BIOLOGICALLY BUILT TO EAT ANIMAL PRODUCTS?

Ah, one of the most common vegan myths! Historical evidence suggests our bodies are not designed to eat meat. Most carnivores in the animal kingdom, such as lions, have sharp claws for catching prey, which we as humans don't possess. Carnivores also have long canine teeth to tear flesh, and jaws which move up and down to trap prey. Human jaws on the other hand, move from side to side (grinding) as well as up and down, whilst we only have small canines and mostly blunted teeth, suggesting we are more suited to vegetable, fruit and seed digestion.

And there's more! Humans consuming raw meat, raw eggs or non-pasteurised milk can become ill, while natural predators have no such problem chowing down on raw gazelle, again suggesting we are not necessarily built to eat animal products.

BISCUITY BANANA BREAD

Now for the fun bit – eating! Why not start your vegan adventure by baking this light and fluffy banana bread, laced with cookie spread and topped with crunchy cookies? Perfect with a cup of tea or as a dessert with ice cream.

INGREDIENTS

3 ripe bananas, mashed
2 tbsp chia seeds
60 ml almond milk
2 tbsp olive oil
2 tbsp syrup
1 tsp almond essence
1 cup coconut sugar
1 tsp baking powder
1 tsp bicarbonate of soda
1 tsp cinnamon
1 cup flour e.g. white, spelt (or half and half/your preferred GF flour)
80 g Biscoff cookie spread (or similar)
4 Biscoff cookies (or similar)

1. Preheat the oven to 160C fan/180C/gas mark 4 and line 1 large or 2 small loaf tins with baking paper.

2. Stir the mashed banana with the chia seeds, almond milk, oil, syrup and almond essence in a large mixing bowl. Leave for 5–10 minutes.

Bananas are a great source of fibre and carbohydrate and supply us with the minerals potassium, vitamin B6 and vitamin C.

3. Add in the coconut sugar, baking powder, bicarbonate of soda, cinnamon and flour and stir to combine (the mixture will be quite thick).

4. Pour half the batter into the 2 small or 1 large loaf tin(s) and then spoon over the Biscoff cookie spread in an even layer. Top with the remaining banana bread batter.

5. Crumble the Biscoff cookies on top of the loaves or loaf and bake for 25–30 minutes for 2 small loaves or 35–40 minutes for 1 larger loaf.

6. Allow to cool on a wire rack in the tin(s) for 10 minutes, remove from the tin(s) and then allow to cool fully on the rack. Store in an airtight container for up to 3 days.

ONE PLANET VEGAN PIZZA

Enjoy a delicious homemade pizza with this planet-friendly vegan recipe.

INGREDIENTS

BASE
4 wholemeal vegan flatbreads, bagels or pittas

SAUCE
200g-can chopped tomatoes (ideally Italian)
1 garlic clove
1 tsp chia seeds
1 tsp dried basil
1 tsp dried oregano

TOPPINGS
75g vegan 'cheeze' of choice
25g diced red onion
25g pulled jackfruit
25g vegan meat substitute of choice (such as faux bac'n and faux chick'n)
2 tbsp barbeque sauce

1. Preheat the oven to 220C fan/240C/gas mark 9.

2. Blend the sauce ingredients in a blender or food processor until lovely and smooth.

3. Place your bread of choice on an oven tray and spread the sauce over it.

4. Mix the toppings together and spread as desired (this is your chance to spell out your name and draw a face!).

5. Finish by topping with cheeze.

6. Place in the oven and cook for 10 minutes, until the cheeze has melted and browned.

SERVE AND ENJOY!

HEALTHY APPLE SLICES

These apple slices are a quick and easy snack to make. Have fun creating different versions with your favourite toppings!

1. Turn the apple on its side. Carefully slice it into 1 cm slices.

2. Use a small spoon to remove the core from your apple slices.

INGREDIENTS

1 apple
Coconut, almond or soya yogurt
Chopped nuts
Your favourite nut or seed butter
Mini chocolate chips
Granola
Cake sprinkles

3. Use a piece of kitchen roll to pat your slices dry.

4. Spread a layer of yogurt over your apple slices.

5. Top with your favourite toppings, and drizzle with nut butter. Yum!

VEGAN TOFU NUGGETS WITH SPICY TOMATO SAUCE

These delicious vegan nuggets are a perfect spicy treat, served hot or cold.

1. Preheat the oven to 170C fan/190C/ gas mark 5 and line a baking tray with baking paper.

2. Pat the tofu dry and cut into about 18 cubes.

3. Place the milk in a shallow bowl.

4. Mix the breadcrumbs, nutritional yeast, turmeric, garlic powder and paprika in a bowl and season with salt and black pepper.

5. Dip the tofu cubes in the milk a few at a time and then place into a sealable bag with some of the nugget coating. Shake the bag to coat the cubes evenly with the nugget mix, and place carefully onto the baking tray. Repeat until all of the cubes are coated. Any leftover coating mix is great sprinkled over salads, pastas and grains.

6. Bake in the oven for 25–30 minutes, or until golden and crisp, turning the cubes over carefully halfway through.

INGREDIENTS

NUGGETS
1 block extra-firm tofu (200 g)
3 tbsp plant-based milk
3 tbsp breadcrumbs
1 tbsp nutritional yeast
1 tsp ground turmeric
1 tsp smoked paprika
1 tsp garlic powder
Salt and black pepper to taste

SPICY TOMATO SAUCE
3 tbsp tomato puree
1 tsp smoked paprika
2 tbsp tamari soy sauce
1 tsp coconut honey or syrup
1 tsp sriracha
1–2 tbsp water, to thin

Tomatoes are usually red but you can also buy yellow, green or purple tomatoes!

7. Meanwhile, make the spicy tomato sauce by mixing together all the ingredients in a small bowl. Taste and adjust the seasoning: more sriracha for heat; more paprika for smokiness; more soy sauce for savoury saltiness or more honey for sweetness.

8. Serve warm with the sauce or leave to cool and enjoy later. These nuggets will keep well in an airtight container in the fridge for up to three days.

Animal sanctuary: An often charitable and independent organisation, run with the intention of allowing abandoned, unwanted or ex-farm animals to live the rest of their lives in their natural habitats, free from harm and exploitation.

Cholesterol: A substance that is found in the bodies of all animals. Too much cholesterol in the blood can cause heart disease.

Deforestation: A clearing of a large area of forest, woodland or area of trees.

Fast fashion: A term used to describe the quickly changing trends in the fashion industry, which lead retailers to produce cheap on-trend clothes, the vast majority of which are in style one minute, and out the next.

Fortified foods: Foods which have been enriched with added vitamins and minerals.

Omnivore: An omnivore is an individual who eats meat, fish, dairy and eggs as well as nuts, seeds, fruits, vegetables and grains. These individuals consume all food groups, animal products included.

Organic: Methods of farming that use natural, rather than chemical products, to help plants or animals to grow.

Plant-based: Plant-based is another way of saying that you choose to eat a vegan diet. Being plant-based doesn't necessarily mean that you'll adhere to the moral and ethical beliefs of living a vegan lifestyle however, rather that you choose not to eat any animal products in your daily diet.

Protein: An important substance that is found in food and is used by our bodies to grow and repair themselves.

Sentient beings: Vegans believe that all animals are sentient beings, in that they have the capacity to feel emotion, recognise and respond to their environment, in the same sense that humans can.

Supplements: Vitamins and minerals that are consumed alongside a (vegan) diet to ensure good health.

Tempeh: A cultured soya-bean product which is high in protein and full of healthy bacteria. You can cook with it in a similar way to tofu.

Tofu: Tofu is made from soya milk, which is condensed and pressed into a block. It is a versatile ingredient, rich in protein as well as calcium.

Veganism: a way of living which seeks to exclude, as far as is possible and practicable, all forms of exploitation of, and cruelty to, animals for food, clothing or any other purpose.

Wholefood plant-based diet: The term used to describe a health-affirming vegan diet. A wholefood plant-based diet consists primarily of wholegrains, beans and pulses, fruits, vegetables, some heathy fats and fortified foods such as plant-based milks and tofu. Processed vegan foods are kept to a minimum.

NON-VEGAN INGREDIENTS

Additives: Certain E numbers are derived from animal products, including E120, E322, E422, E417.

Bee products: This includes honey, bee propolis and royal jelly (in beauty products), beeswax and bee pollen.

Carmine: Carmine (also known as cochineal) is a red food, textile and cosmetic dye colouring made from crushed beetles.

Casein: Derived from milk.

Gelatine: Animal-based gelatine is often used in certain sweets and baked goods. Animal-based gelatine is made from animal skin and/or bone, and is therefore not considered to be a part of a vegan diet.

Ghee (unless stated as vegetable): This is also derived from milk and is sometimes used as a cooking oil.

Lactose: Derived from milk.

Lard: An animal fat.

Omega-3 fatty acids (not specified origin): Many of these products will not be vegan, as they will contain ingredients derived from fish.

Rennet: Produced from the stomach of mammals, is sometimes used as a processing aid in foods.

Shellac: Created from an insect, this is used as a shiny cover on certain sweets and sometimes forms a wax coating on lemons and citrus fruits.

Tallow: An animal fat.

Whey: Derived from milk.

FIND OUT MORE

CHARITIES FOR GENERAL ADVICE AND NUTRITIONAL GUIDANCE:
www.vegansociety.com
https://www.vegansociety.com/go-vegan/how-go-vegan
www.veganuary.com
www.viva.org.uk
www.animalaid.org.uk

RECIPE RESOURCES:
www.nourishingamy.com
www.bosh.tv
www.exceedinglyvegan.com
www.forksoverknives.com
www.nutritionxkitchen.com
www.veganfoodandliving.com
https://www.vegansociety.com/resources/recipes

CRUELTY-FREE BEAUTY
www.crueltyfreekitty.com
www.leapingbunny.org

DOCUMENTARIES
The Game Changers
What The Health
Vegucated

ABOUT THE AUTHOR:
Charlotte Willis is an author, writer, editor and content creator whose interests and work promote sustainable living and purpose, in every sense of the word. Charlotte has been actively involved in the UK's vegan scene and the plant-based industry for just over six years, writing for ethically-minded publications and blogs, working for vegan charitable organisations such as Veganuary and The Vegan Society, and coordinating marketing and social media for forward-thinking, ethical brands. A passionate advocate of women's mental health, Charlotte is currently pursuing an MSc in clinical psychology, with the view to revolutionising women's holistic healthcare. Find Charlotte on **Instagram:** @charlottesophiewrites

CONTRIBUTORS

ONE PLANET PIZZA

One Planet Pizza are an ethical family-run business based in Norwich, Norfolk. Their mission is to make this world a better place, one slice at a time, and they believe that food should be delicious, healthy and sustainable, without compromise. One Planet Pizza are the UK's first vegan frozen pizza company, and use all-natural ingredients in their delicious award-winning pizzas. You can even buy their pizzas direct from their website for delivery to your home!

Website: www.oneplanetpizza.com
Social media: www.instagram.com/oneplanetpizza

AMY LANZA

Amy is a plant-based food blogger, recipe developer, content creator and food stylist, creating and sharing vegan recipes to nourish your soul and body, alongside inspirational messages. Eating and living the Nourishing Amy way is to be in tune with your body's natural rhythm, to listen to its cravings and to treat each meal as a special occasion – to nourish you from the inside out. *Nourish Me: 12 Everyday Recipes for Delicious Plant-Based Living*, is Amy's first ebook. It features 12 new plant-based recipes to help you to add some more vegetables, fruit and wholesome treats into your everyday life. The recipes are simple to follow with easy-to-find ingredients. They are all naturally gluten-free or have gluten-free options to suit everyone.

Website: nourishingamy.com/ and nourishingamy.com/ebook
Social media: www.instagram.com/nourishing.amy/

MICAH SIVA

Micah is a registered dietician and a certified chef, focusing on creating high-quality recipes that can be made and created at home. Micah's philosophy is that "Nutrition starts in the kitchen. Food should be enjoyed, with others, with passion and care. Eat what makes your mind and body feel its best". Micah is also a published author of a children's book on diabetes and nutrition, called *A Small Part Of Me: Diabetes*.

Website: www.nutritionxkitchen.com
Social media: www.instagram.com/nutritionxkitchen

INDEX